Watch me grow
Rabbit

TED SMART

LONDON, NEW YORK, MUNICH,
MELBOURNE, and DELHI

Written and edited by Lisa Magloff
Designed by Sonia Whillock,
Mary Sandberg, and Pilar Morales

Publishing Manager Sue Leonard
Managing Art Editor Clare Shedden
Jacket Design Simon Oon
Picture Researcher Sarah Stewart-Richardson
Production Shivani Pandey
DTP Designer Almudena Díaz

This edition published in 2007 by Dorling Kindersley Limited,
80 Strand, London WC2R 0RL

This edition produced for The Book People Ltd,
Hall Wood Avenue, Haydock, St Helens WA11 9UL

First published in Great Britain in 2004 by
Dorling Kindersley Limited
80 Strand, London WC2R 0RL

A Penguin Company

ISBN 978-1-4053-2600-1

Colour reproduction by
Media, Development and Printing, Ltd.
Printed and bound by
Star Standard PTE LTD, Singapore

see our complete catalogue at

www.dk.com

Contents

I'm a rabbit

I have two large ears and a fluffy tail. My strong back legs help me to leap and run, and I am covered in soft fur to keep me warm.

A great sense of smell helps rabbits to sniff out danger.

Strong claws are good for digging.

This is my family.

Rabbits have many layers of thick fur.

Running away

Rabbits can run about as fast as you can ride your bicycle. This helps them outrun their enemies.

Wake up everyone, it's time to get hopping.

My mum and dad

My mum and dad made their home under a large tree. They live with other rabbit families in a series of underground tunnels called a warren.

This is Dad.

This is Mum.

Saying hello
When rabbits meet they say hello to each other by sniffing and touching noses.

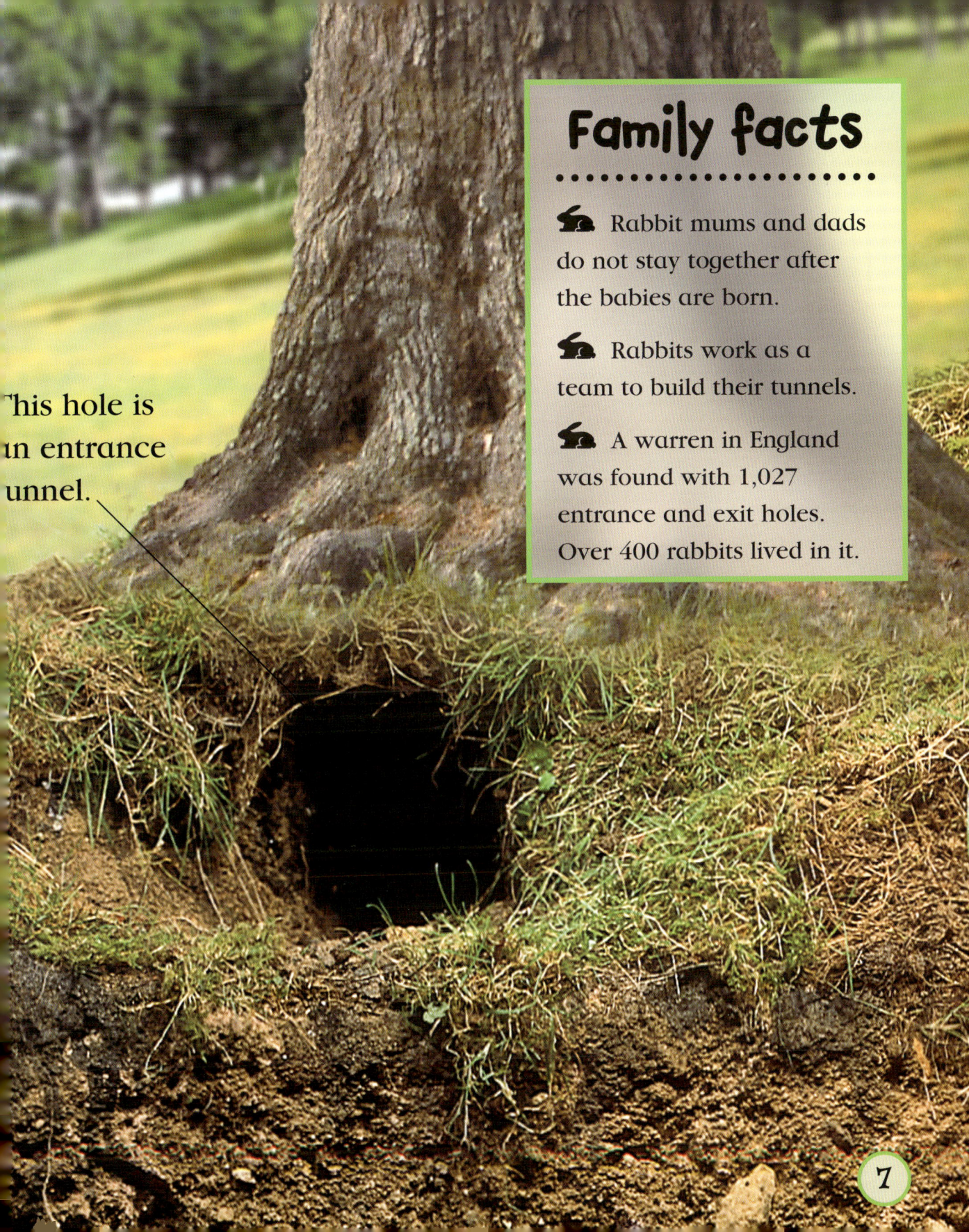

This hole is an entrance tunnel.

Family facts

- 🐇 Rabbit mums and dads do not stay together after the babies are born.

- 🐇 Rabbits work as a team to build their tunnels.

- 🐇 A warren in England was found with 1,027 entrance and exit holes. Over 400 rabbits lived in it.

Here is my home

After they meet, Mum and Dad dig a big, cosy chamber where we will be born. This is our nest.

Shopping trip

Up on the surface, rabbits collect grass, feathers, and fur to make a soft nest.

Can you see the cosy bed Mum has made?

I'm on the lookout.

The warren is a safe place to live. Larger animals find it hard to **squeeze** through the tunnels.

Inside my family's nest

When I am born, my eyes are shut tight and I don't have any fur. We stay warm by huddling close together in the cosy nest Mum has built.

Day one... **day two...**

day three.

Now I'm two weeks old.

All grow bigger!
At first the bunnies are very weak. They can hardly move at all. But soon they can move around. After 10 days they open their eyes.

Lullaby bunny
When they are not eating, the babies sleep for almost all of the time. Growing fast is very tiring.

After two weeks, the bunnies have thick fur and they spend more time awake.

I'm getting curious

After about three weeks
we like to run and jump
around inside the warren.
We can't wait to start
exploring the big
world outside.

Mother's milk

Mother rabbits feed
their baby bunnies
with milk. This is
called nursing. The
bunnies are fed only
once each day.

Rabbit facts

🐰 Rabbits spend most of their day undeground. They come out to eat at sunset and at dawn.

🐰 Rabbits can hear many sounds that humans cannot.

🐰 The deepest warren tunnels ever found were dug 9 metres (27 ft) underground.

Now the bunnies are full and sleepy.

I'm four weeks old

It's time for me to hop out of my burrow. My brothers and sisters and I stay close to the entrance, just in case we need to **ZO**ooom back inside!

Rabbits' ears stick up high to listen for danger.

The warm sand is a comfy place for the rabbits to sit.

I'm so shy, I think I'll hide!

Take care!

Outside the safety of the warren, the bunnies are always on the lookout for danger. Bunnies are a meal for animals like eagles, foxes, and weasels.

eagle

fox

It's back down the tunnel when we get a fright!

The bunny's eyes quickly get used to bright daylight.

I can find my own dinner

Now I am old enough to look for food on my own. Green, leafy plants are my favourite food. I find yummy plants to eat growing in fields and in gardens.

This looks like a good place to eat dinner.

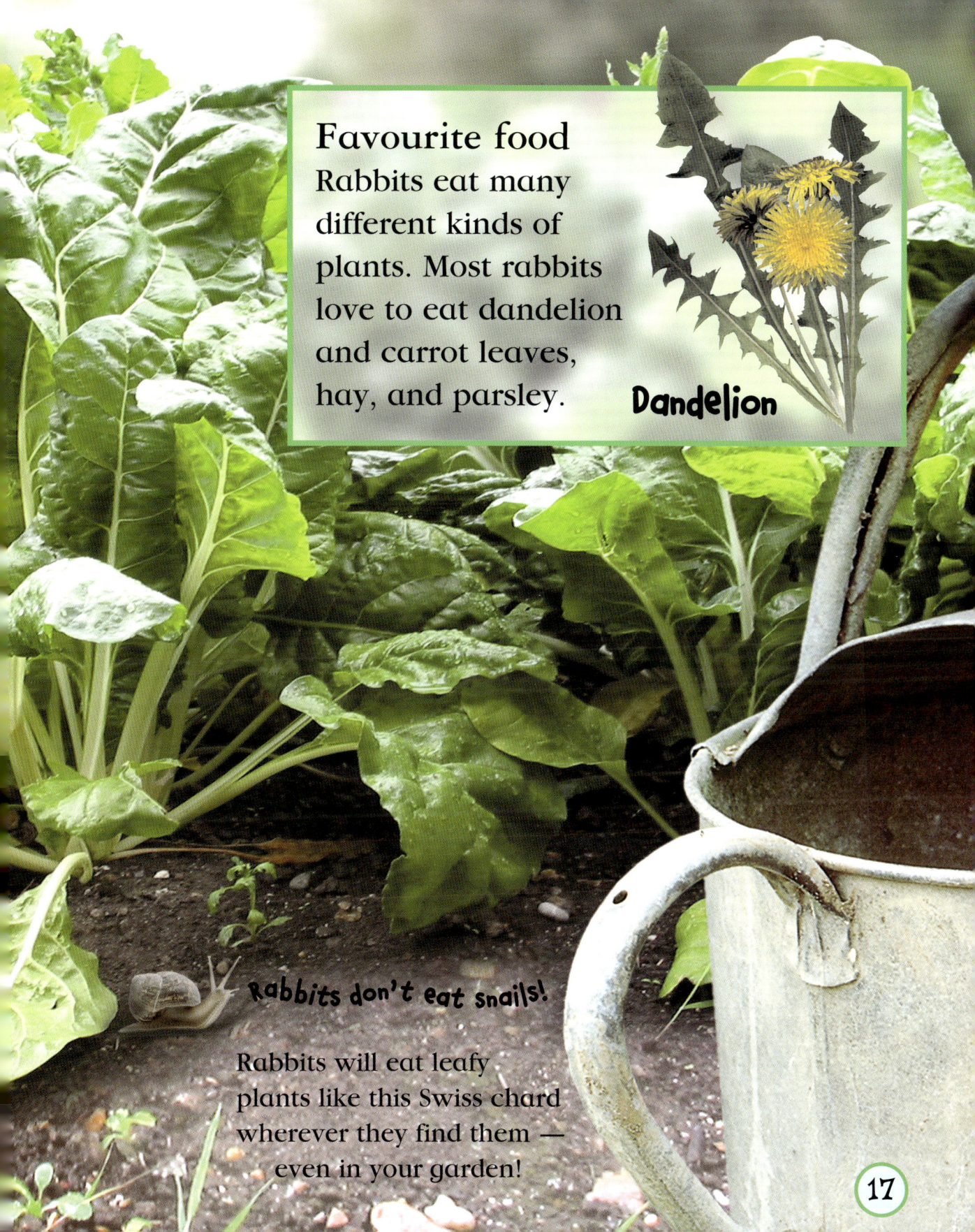

Favourite food

Rabbits eat many different kinds of plants. Most rabbits love to eat dandelion and carrot leaves, hay, and parsley.

Dandelion

Rabbits don't eat snails!

Rabbits will eat leafy plants like this Swiss chard wherever they find them — even in your garden!

Now I'm grown up

After just eight weeks I am all grown up. I spend my time running in the fields, looking for good things to eat. Soon it will be time to start a family of my own.

Rabbits smell plants to see if they are good to eat.

Bath time
Rabbits spend a lot of time washing their fur. This is called grooming.

The rabbits' noses
tell them that these
buttercups are not
good to eat.

Family life
Adult rabbits live
together in a group.
When new rabbits
are born, they stay
in the group.

The circle of life goes round and round

Now you know how I turned into a grown-up rabbit.

Bye bye, off I hop.

My friends from around the world

Can you see why this rabbit is called a Blue dwarf ?

The Jackrabbit lives in the desert. Its big ears help it to stay cool in the desert sun.

This Angora rabbit has a lot of fur, and even funny tufts of fur on the tips of its ears!

The mountain hare has huge feet, which help it to run in the snow

My fluffy, furry rabbit friends come in all sizes and colours.

Dutch rabbits are one of the most popular pet rabbits. They are known for being very gentle.

Lop-eared rabbits have ears that flop down to the ground.

The tiny pika is the size of a hamster!

The Lion-head rabbit has a mane of fur on top of its head.

The Mountain hare is white so its enemies can't see it in the snow.

Rabbit facts

🐰 A rabbit's teeth grow throughout its entire life. Rabbits need to chew wood to keep their teeth short.

🐰 When rabbits are happy they like to jump around and leap about.

🐰 Rabbits are the most active at dawn and at twilight.

Glossary

Warren
A system of underground tunnels that rabbits live in.

Claw
A sharp nail on the rabbit's toe that helps the rabbit to dig.

Nest
A place inside the warren where rabbit babies are born.

Kitten
The name for a baby rabbit that is less than one month old.

Litter
A group of baby rabbits all born to the same mother.

Grooming
When the rabbit washes its fur to keep it clean and free of bugs.

Acknowledgements

The publisher would like to thank the following for their kind permission to reproduce their photographs:
(Key: a=above; c=centre; b=below; l=left; r=right; t=top)
1 Warren Photographic: Jane Burton c, bl. 2-3 Bruce Coleman Ltd: William S. Paton bkg&c. 2 DK Images: Jane Burton b. 3 Oxford Scientific Films: Jorge Sierra Antinolo br. 4-5 DK Images: Geoff Dann. 4 DK Images: Dave King l; Steven Moore Photography r; Bruce Coleman Ltd: William S. Paton b. 5 Bruce Coleman Ltd: William S. Paton br; FLPA - Images of nature: David Hosking tr; Steven Moore Photography tl; Warren Photographic: Jane Burton bl. 6-7 Corbis: Terry W. Eggers t; DK Images: Steve Shott b; 6 DK Images: Steve Shott c; Jane Burton cr; Bruce Coleman Ltd: Colin Varndell bl. 7 Corbis: Phillip Gould tc. 8-9 Corbis: Terry W. Eggers t; DK Images: Steve Shott b. 8 Corbis: Phillip Gould; Oxford Scientific Films cl. 9 DK Images: Steve Shott tlb. 10-11 Oxford Scientific Films.10 Bruce Coleman Ltd: Jane Burton tl, c; Warren Photographic: Jane Burton tr. 11 Bruce Coleman Ltd: Jane Burton tr. 12 DK Images: Steve Shott l. 12-13 Oxford Scientific Films: Maurice Tibbles. 14-15 Bruce Coleman Ltd: William S. Paton. 15 DK Images: Frank Greenaway rca; Jerry Young rc; Oxford Scientific Films: br. 16-17 Steven Moore Photography. 16 DK Images: Ian O'Leary l; FLPA - Images of nature: Tony Hamblin br. 17 Royalty Free Images: Photofrenetic/ Alamy tr; DK Images: Jacqui Hurst br. 18-19 Bruce Coleman Ltd: Colin Varndell. 18 FLPA - Images of nature: Tony Hamblin br. 19 Oxford Scientific Films: Mike Powles tr. 20 Bruce Coleman Ltd: Jane Burton tc, trb; Corbis: Tony Hamblin bl; DK Images: Barrie Watts bc; Geoff Dann tl; Jane Burton cl; Warren Photographic: Jane Burton tr, cr, crb, c. 21 Steven Moore Photography bkg; Oxford Scientific Films: Jorge Sierra Antinolo c. 22 DK Images: Jane Burton tl; Steve Shott cl; Oxford Scientific Films: Paul Berquist tr; Warren Photographic: Jane Burton c. 22-23 Powerstock: Superstock. 23 Corbis: George D. Lepp trb; DK Images: Steve Shott tr; FLPA - Images of nature: Terry Whittaker cla; Steven Moore Photography: br; Warren Photographic: Jane Burton cl. 24 Bruce Coleman Ltd: Jane Burton cr, bl; DK Images: Steve Shott tl, cl; Steven Moore Photography: tr.
All other images © Dorling Kindersley.
For further information see: www.dkimages.com